M000074691

Something to Think About . . .

Did you know?

* There are more than 200 billion billion stars.

* Stars are made mostly of hydrogen and helium.

Why can't we see stars during the day?

Why are stars different colors?

Have you ever seen a falling star? It really isn't a star at all. It's a *meteor*. A meteor is a piece of metal or rock that burns up as it falls through the air.

Stars
Near & Far

by Robin Dexter

illustrated by Susan T. Hall

Troll Associates

LIBRARY OF CONGRESS CATALOGING-IN-PUBLICATION DATA

Dexter, Robin.
   Stars / by Robin Dexter ; illustrated by Susan T. Hall.
     p.   cm. — (First-start science)
   Summary: Provides basic facts about the stars and constellations.
   ISBN 0-8167-3858-0 (lib. bdg.) — ISBN 0-8167-3859-9 (pbk.)
1. Astronomy—Juvenile literature. 2. Astronomy—Pictorial works —
Juvenile literature. 3. Stars—Juvenile literature. 4. Stars—Pictorial
works—Juvenile literature. [1. Astronomy. 2. Stars.] I. Hall, Susan
T., ill. II. Title. III. Series: Troll first-start science.
QB46.D49   1996
523.8—dc20   95-4869

See the stars shine in the night sky?
How beautiful they are!

Did you know we can also see
a star shine during the day?
That star is our sun.

Every day our Earth turns around.
When our side of Earth faces the
sun, it is day.

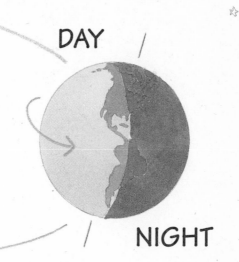

DAY

NIGHT

It is so bright, we cannot
see the other stars.

When our side of Earth turns away from
the sun, it is night. That is when we can
see the other stars.

Our Earth also spins around the sun.
The sun and the planets that spin
around it form our solar system.

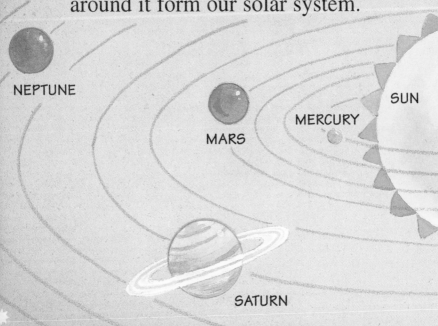

NEPTUNE

MARS

MERCURY

SUN

SATURN

Stars are *very* big.
They look small because they
are far, far away from Earth.

The sun is the closest star to Earth. It would take a rocket ship about 155 days to reach our sun. It would take a rocket ship about 42 million days to reach the next closest star!

Our sun and Earth are part of a big family of stars and their planets.

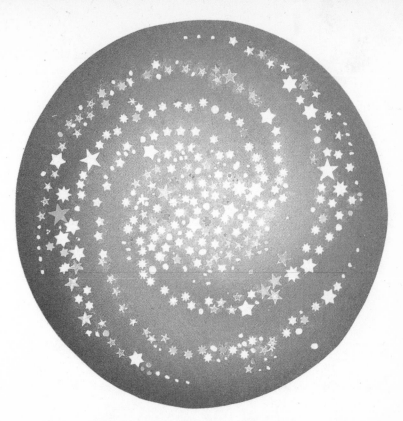

This family is called
the Milky Way galaxy.

Did you know stars
are fiery balls of gas?
They are hot!

Feel the heat from our sun?
The sun's heat warms the earth.

Stars have colors, too.
The sun is a yellow-orange star.

SUN

Blue stars are hotter than the sun.

RIGEL   BETELGEUSE

Red stars are not as hot as the sun.

Look at the night sky.

Do some stars look like
pictures of people or things?

Groups of stars that look like
pictures are called constellations.

This constellation is called Orion.

Orion was a mighty hunter in stories told long ago.

Can you find this constellation
in the night sky? It looks like
a pot with a long handle.
Yes! It's the Big Dipper.

Look! There goes a falling star. Falling stars are not really stars at all. They are actually meteors.

A meteor is a piece of metal or rock in space. It burns as it falls through the air.

How many stars are there?
Billions and billions!
And new ones are always forming.

See the stars shine?
How beautiful they are!